254 Cool Facts You Probably Never Knew

I0102167

Liam Willis

Tiff, ink. Publications - Dallas

DEDICATION

This book is dedicated to my sister, Frannie Willis. She taught me how to read before I was in kindergarten. She's been there for me for my entire life, and I wouldn't be who I am without her.

CHAPTER 1: TOYS

1. If Barbie were a real woman, her measurements would be 39-inch bust, 18-inch waist, and 33-inch hips. Her neck would be too small to support her head.

2. The original hack-sack was invented in Turkey.

3. Barbie's full name is Barbara Millicent Roberts.

4. Barbie's boyfriend is Ken Carson.

5. Barbie's parents are George and Margaret Roberts, and they live in Willows, Wisconsin.

6. A Chinese checker board has 121 holes.

7. There are 43,252,003,274,489,856,000 (43 quintillion) possible color combinations on a Rubik's Cube.

8. LEGO is the world's number one manufacturer of tires because over half of all Lego sets have tires.

9. A Slinky is made of 63 feet of wire.

10. McDonald's restaurants are the world's largest distributor of toys.

11. Mr. Potato Head was the first toy ever advertised on TV.

12. The Yo-Yo was used as a weapon beginning about the year 1500 in the Philippine Islands.

CHAPTER 2: TV

13. Kermit the Frog is left-handed. Actually, most Muppets are left-handed.

14. The reason is that the Muppeteer always holds the Muppet above his head or in front of his body. One hand operates the head and mouth and the other hand manipulates the hands and arms. Because of this, the Muppeteer uses his right hand to operate the head and his left hand to operate the arm rod.

15. Gilligan of "Gilligan's Island" had a first name that was used only one time on the show, and it was the pilot show (first show) that wasn't ever on TV. His name was Willy.

16. The Skipper's real name was Jonas Grumby. It was mentioned one time in the first episode on the radio newscast they listened to about the wreck.

17. On Gilligan's Island, the Professor's real name was Roy Hinkley. Mary Ann's last name was Summers. Mrs. Howell's maiden name was Wentworth.

18. Popeye has four nephews and their names are Pipeye, Peepeye, Pupeye, and Poopeye.

19. The Muppet Show" is banned from Saudi Arabian television because one if its stars, Miss Piggy, is a pig. Miss Piggy merchandise is seized from shops and destroyed. The Prophet Muhammad declared the "flesh of swine" an "abomination.

20. One in every four Americans has been on TV.

21. If all episodes of the "The Simpsons" were watched back to back without stopping, it would take a week to watch them all.

22. In the cartoon The Jetsons, Jane Jetson was 32 and her daughter Judy was 16. That means Jane was a teen mom.

23. Robin Williams ,Tom Cruise, Gene Hackman, and Dr.Seuss

were all voted "Least Likely To Succeed" by their classmates.

24. The "Think Music" that's played in Jeopardy's final round was written by Merv Griffin, the creator of the show.

25. Kelsey Grammar sings and plays the piano for the theme song of his TV show, Fraiser.

CHAPTER 3: MOVIES

26. The cost of filming of the movie Titanic was more than the cost of the Titanic itself. The film cost $200 million dollars, and the cost to build the Titanic was about $120-$150 million dollars.

27. Sean Connery turned down the role of Gandalf in Lord of the Rings because he didn't understand the part. He could have made $450 million dollars.

28. The name for Oz in The Wizard of Oz was made up when the movie's creator, Frank Baum, glanced up at his filing cabinet and saw the letters A-N on one drawer, and O-Z on the next drawer.

29. All of the clocks in the movie "Pulp Fiction" are stuck on 4:20.

30. The mask worn by Michael Myers in the original Halloween movie was actually a Captain Kirk Star Trek mask painted white.

31. In the original version of Cinderella the slipper was made of fur, not glass.

32. C3PO was the very first character to speak in Star Wars when he said "What was that?".

33. The creators of Star Wars modeled Yoda's face after Stuart Freeborn, the makeup supervisor for "Star Wars". He added Albert Einstein's eyes and wrinkles to give Yoda a "wise look".

34. Albert Einstein's face was the inspiration for E.T.

35. In the movie The Wizard Of Oz, Toto, Dorothy's dog, earned $125 a week, and Judy Garland earned $500 a week. The midgets made $50 dollars per week.

36. In the Mel Brooks film, Silent Movie, the famous mime Marcel Marceau is the only person with a speaking role. A mime is someone who never speaks. But in this movie, he

said "Non!" which is German for "no".

37.   Silent Movie is listed in the Guinness Book of World Records as having the fewest spoken lines in a sound movie.

CHAPTER 4: CANDY

CHOCOLATE

38. Jelly beans didn't become an Easter tradition until the 1930's.

39. Jelly beans were first made during the Civil War in America by Boston candy maker William Schraft. He ran ads to encourage people to send them to soldiers.

40. During World War II, chocolate became more expensive and people started buying jelly beans instead.

41. Jelly beans probably became associated with Eater because of their egg shape.

42. Jelly beans were President Ronald Reagan's favorite treat.

43. The Tootsie Roll was introduced in 1896 by Leo Hirshfield, an Austrian immigrant to the United States. He started a candy business in a small New York City shop. He wanted a candy that wouldn't melt in the heat. He invented a cheap alternative chocolate, the Tootsie Roll.

44. The Tootsie Roll was named them after Leo Hirshfield's daughter. Her nickname was "Tootsie".

45. The Snickers bar, introduced in 1930 by M&M/Mars, is named after Snickers, the Mars family's favorite horse.

46. "Baby Ruth" candy bars was first sold in 1920. It is named after President Grover Cleveland's daughter, not legendary baseball player Babe Ruth.

47. The original 3 Musketeers Bar was introduced in 1932 and had had three parts in every package: chocolate, strawberry, and vanilla. That's why it's called "3 Musketeers."

48. It was Nestle who first introduced chocolate chips in 1939.

49. The cacao tree, native to South America, produces the seeds that are the source of cocoa and chocolate.

50. The first recorded case of "Death by Chocolate" occurred in

the 17th century in Mexico. The Bishop of Chiapas was poisoned by an angry town lady.

51. Hershey's Kisses were introduced in 1907. They are one of the best selling chocolates and Hershey produces approximately 20-25 million Kisses per day..

52. In 1913, a process was invented by a Swiss Confectioner named Jules Sechaud that allowed chocolates to have unique fillings.

Liam Willis

CHAPTER 5: SPORTS

53. The first baseball caps were made out of straw.

54. Tug-of-war was an Olympic event between 1900 and 1920.

55. The New York Yankees started the practice of identifying baseball players by number in 1929.

56. In Thailand kite flying is a professional sport.

57. It takes 3,000 cows to supply the NFL with enough leather for a year's supply of footballs.

58. All major league baseball umpires must wear black underwear while on the job in case their pants split.

59. The average life span of a major league baseball is five to seven pitches.

60. Prior to 1900, boxing prize fights lasted up to 100 rounds.

61. Babe Ruth wore number 3 because he batted third.

62. During World War II, when many Major League Baseball players were called to military duty, the Pittsburgh Steelers and Philadelphia Eagles combined to become The Steagles.

CHAPTER 6: ANIMALS

63.   Hippo milk is pink.

64.   A few species of turtles can breathe through their butts.

65.   Crocodiles can't stick out their tongues.

66.   The Bee Hummingbird, or Zunzuncito, weighs less than penny.

67.   Parrot parents "name" their children with a signature call.

68.   A giraffe's kick is powerful enough to decapitate a lion.

69.   Moths are unable to fly during an earthquake.

70.   A single breath from a mature blue whale can inflate up to 2,000 balloons.

71.   Gorillas can catch human colds and other illnesses.

72.   The sound of a tiger's roar can travel a distance of up to two miles.

CHAPTER 7: CELEBRITIES

73.   Annie Edson-Taylor was the first person to go over Niagara falls. She made the trip in a wooden barrel and survived.

74.   Thomas Edison, the inventor of the light bulb, was afraid of the dark.

75.   If you rearrange the letters in Vin Diesel's name, it reveals his credo: "I End Lives."

76.   Elvis had a twin who died.

77.   Oprah Winfrey makes $10 per second.

78.   Ian McKellen and Patrick Stewart did not know how to play chess when they appeared in X-Men 2.

79.   When he was a child, Jim Carrey wore tap shoes to bed in case his parents needed cheering up in the middle of the night.

80.   The trucking company Elvis Presley worked for as a young man was owned by Frank Sinatra

CHAPTER 8: WEATHER

81. In 1932, the winter was so cold that Niagara Falls froze completely solid.

82. Dirty snow melts faster than clean snow does.

83. Oak trees are struck by lightning more often than any other tree.

84. In ten minutes, a hurricane releases more energy than all the world's nuclear weapons combined.

85. Nine out of ten lightning strike victims survive.

86. The speed of a typical raindrop is 17 miles per hour.

87. Rain contains vitamin B12.

88. It is possible to see a rainbow at night.

89. Contrary to popular belief, lightning travels from the ground upwards, not from the sky downwards.

90. Men are six times more likely to be struck by lightning than women.

Liam Willis

CHAPTER 9: SPACE

91. Only 55% of Americans know that the sun is a star.

92. If two pieces of metal touch in space, they become permanently stuck together.

93. There are two golf balls sitting on the moon.

94. The planet Earth gets 100 tons heavier every day because of falling space dust.

95. It would take more than 150 years to drive a car to the sun.

96. An unprotected human being can survive up to one and a half minutes in space with no permanent bodily damage.

97. Summer on Uranus lasts for 21 years.

98. Sound doesn't travel in space.

99. Jupiter is bigger than all of the other planets combined.

100. Astronauts' hearts become smaller when they are in outer space.

CHAPTER 10: HISTORY

101. Vikings used the skulls of their enemies to drink out of.

102. The first coast-to-coast telephone line was established in1914.

103. Until President John F. Kennedy was killed, it wasn't a federal crime to assassinate a President.

104. In 1537, England's King Henry VII officially declared February 14th as Saint Valentine's Day.

105. There is no documented evidence that prove that pirates made people walk the plank.

106. In Ancient Egypt, many people paid their taxes in honey.

107. Two of the survivors from the Titanic were dogs.

108. In 1447, Leonardo Da Vinci predicted the mass use of solar energy.

CHAPTER 11: POLITICS

> We chose to go to the moon in this decade and do the other things, not because they are easy, but because they are hard.
>
> **John F. Kennedy**

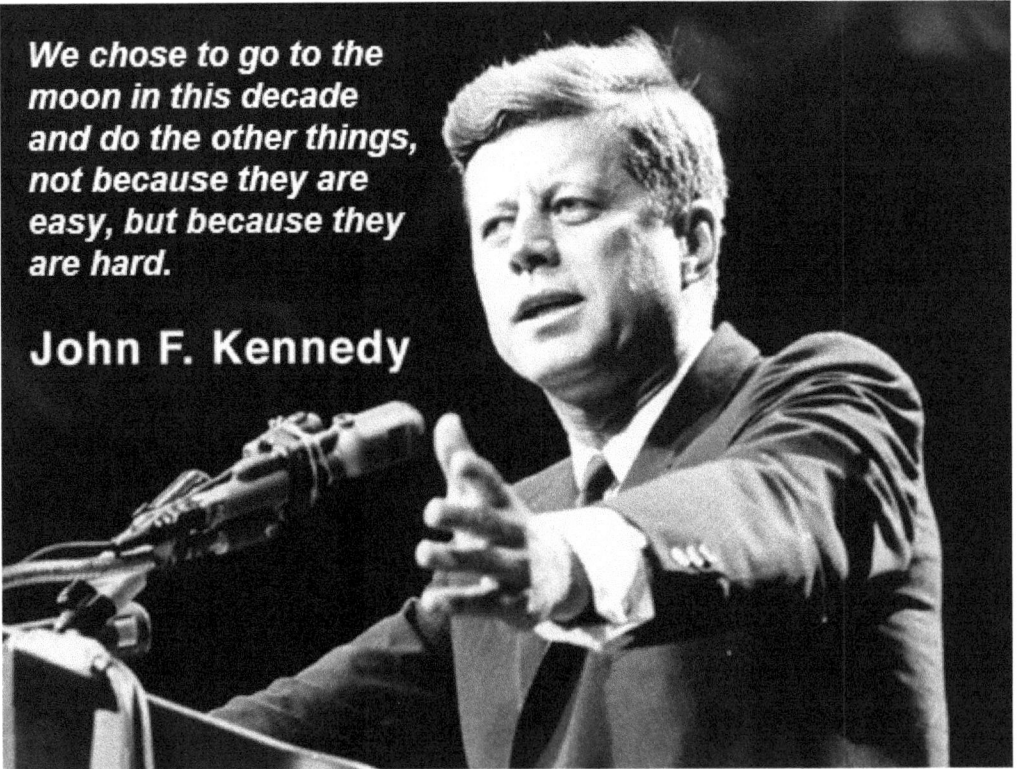

109. Abraham Lincoln was a licensed bartender.

110. George W. Bush was the head of the cheerleading team when he was in high school.

111. Jimmy Carter was the first President of the United States to be born in a hospital.

112. In 1789, the total United States federal government debt was $190,000.

113. Every United States president with a beard has been a Republican.

114. George Washington grew marijuana plants in his garden.

115. So far, no President of the United States was an only child.

116. President George W. Bush and Playboy founder Hugh Hefner are cousins.

117. The system of democracy was introduced 2,500 years ago in Athens, Greece.

118. President Lyndon B. Johnson smoked at least three packs of cigarettes per day.

Liam Willis

CHAPTER 12: HUMANS

119. Studies have shown that blue-eyed people have a higher tolerance for alcohol.

120. Studies suggest that laziness is a natural part of being a teenager and doesn't mean that someone has bad behavior.

121. 44% of kids watch television before they go to sleep.

122. People forget 90% of their dreams.

123. Two out of five people in the world end up marrying their first love.

124. According to a study conducted in the United Kingdom, women are better at parking cars than men are.

125. 91% of Americans eat turkey on Thanksgiving Day.

126. Most babies crawl an average of 200 meters per day.

127. Women who use lipstick use their height in lipstick every five years.

128. Dutch people, on average are the tallest people.

Liam Willis

CHAPTER 13: STATES AND COUNTRIES

129. The province of Alberta, Canada doesn't have the common rat in their province.

130. The United States has paved enough roads to circle the globe over 150 times.

131. Denmark has twice as many pigs as people.

132. The Statue of Liberty wears a size 879 shoe.

133. Canada has more lakes than the rest of the world combined.

134. Almost half the newspapers in the world are published in the United States and Canada.

135. Every year, 203 million dollars are spent on barbed wire in the United States.

136. Windmills always turn counter-clockwise, except for the windmills in Ireland.

137. Wyoming was the first state to give women the right to vote.

138. The United States consumes 25 percent of all the world's energy.

CHAPTER 14: CHRISTMAS

139. One town in Indiana is called Santa Claus. There is also a Santa, Idaho.

140. Coca Cola was the first beverage company to use Santa Claus for a winter advertisement.

141. 7.6 million Christmas trees are sold every year

142. Nearly 60 million Christmas trees are grown each year in Europe.

143. The world's tallest Christmas tree was 221 feet tall and was erected in a Washington shopping mall in 1950.

144. The tradition of giving gold-wrapped chocolate coins began with Saint Nicholas, who gave bags of gold coins to poor people.

145. Electric lights for Christmas trees were first used in 1895.

146. Boxing Day is called boxing day because it was the day families opened gift boxes for poor people.

147. Scientists calculated that Santa would have to visit 822 homes per second to deliver all the world's presents on Christmas Eve.

148. To accomplish the above feat, this would mean that Santa is traveling at 650 miles per second.

149. Theologians estimate that Jesus was born either in September or sometime in late summer, not on December 25th.

CHAPTER 15: COMPUTERS AND INTERNET

150. Because they want to find any security problems that exist, Facebook pays at least $500 to people who can find a way to hack their site.

151. The domain name www.youtube.com was registered on February 14, 2005.

152. On an average work day for people who type all day, their fingers travel 12.6 miles.

153. The word TYPEWRITER is the longest word that can be made using the letters only on one row of a keyboard.

154. The first banner advertising was used in 1994.

155. In 2011, one of every eight married couples in the United States met online.

156. YouTube is the second most popular search engine in the world.

157. People in China don't have access to Facebook or Google.

158. Apple was created in Steve Job's parents garage.

159. By 2012, there will be approximately 17 billion devices connected to the Internet.

160. Steve Jobs was adopted. His biological father is from Syria.

161. Because of a long rivalry between Microsoft and Apple, Bill Gates' children aren't allowed to have Apple devices such as iPads, iPhones, and iPods.

162. The Bill Gates home was designed using an Apple computer: the Macintosh.

163. A nickname for a Microsoft Windows tutorial is Crash Course.

Liam Willis

CHAPTER 16: THE BUSINESS WORLD

164. The first owner of the Marlboro Tobacco Company died of lung cancer.

165. The famous Marlboro man also died of lung cancer.

166. Dell Computers was started by a 19-year-old with only $1,000.

167. Colgate's first toothpaste came in a jar.

168. The founder of McDonald's has a Bachelor degree in Hamburgerology.

169. Amazon sells more e-books than printed books.

170. All three of the founders of Apple worked at Atari before forming Apple.

171. Bill Gates, the founder of Microsoft, and Steve Jobs, the founder of Apple, were college drop-outs.

172. In Australia, Burger King is called Hungry Jack's.

173. The first product made by Sony was the rice cooker.

174. Duracell, the battery-maker, built some parts of its international headquarters using materials from its own waste.

CHAPTER 17: COOL FACTS ABOUT HEALTH

175. Most women have a better sense of smell than men have.

176. When you take a single step, you are using up to 200 muscles.

177. Dogs can be trained to identify the scent of lung cancer long before symptoms develop.

178. Staying awake for 17 hours has the same effect on your body as drinking 2 glasses of wine.

179. Chewing gum boosts your brain power because it increases mood and alertness.

180. The human brain stops growing when a person is 18 years old.

181. Your thumb is about the same size as your nose.

182. Poor eyesight (myopia) is associated with higher IQ.

183. A person can live without food for about a month, but only about a week without water.

184. After age 30, the brain begins to shrink a quarter of a percent (0.25%) in mass every year.

CHAPTER 18: COOL FACTS ABOUT SCIENCE

185. The only letter that doesn't appear on the Periodic Table of Elements is the letter "J."

186. The human brain consists of 80 percent water.

187. Sound travels about four times faster in water than it travels in air.

188. Scientists aren't sure what color dinosaurs were.

189. The sun is 330,000 times larger than the earth.

190. Out of all the senses, smell is most closely linked to memory.

191. No matter how cold it gets, gasoline will not freeze.

192. One 75-watt bulb gives more light than three 25-watt bulbs.

193. Most dust particles in your house are made from dead skin.

194. Blood sucking hookworms live inside about 700 million people worldwide.

CHAPTER 19: FARTS

195. Termites are the largest producers of farts.

196. Farts are flammable.

197. The word "fart" comes from the Old English "feortan," which means "to break wind."

198. Farts have been clocked at a speed of 10 feet per second.

199. Scuba divers cannot pass gas at depths of 33 feet or below.

200. An average person farts 14 times per day.

201. Excess gas in the intestines is medically termed "flatulence."

202. Although they won't admit it, women fart as much as men.

203. If you fart consistently for six years and nine months, enough gas is produced to create the energy of an atomic bomb.

204. The temperature of a fart at time of creation is the temperature of the human body, usually 98.6 degrees Fahrenheit.

CHAPTER 20: DRINKS

205. Blueberry juice reportedly helps to improve memory.

206. The recipe for beer is the world's oldest known recipe.

207. Dark chocolate contains substances that reduce the risk of heart disease.

208. White wine gets darker in color with age and red wine gets lighter in color.

209. Orange juice contains a small amount of alcohol. Alcohol isn't added to juice. It's produced by the fermentation that happens when yeasts and bacteria convert sugar to carbon dioxide and alcohol.

210. There are about 100,000 bacteria in one liter of drinking water.

211. Wine will spoil if exposed to light, which is why the bottles of many wines are tinted.

212. The original Coca-Cola, from 1885 to 1903, contained Coca, whose active ingredient is cocaine.

213. Pepsi originally contained an ingredient called pepsin, which is where the name "Pepsi" came from.

CHAPTER 21: FOOD

214. Ice Cream was originally a Chinese food.

215. Every month, approximately nine out of ten American children visit McDonald's restaurant.

216. 50 years ago Cheerios were called Cheerioats.

217. America's favorite pizza topping is pepperoni. 50 percent of pizzas ordered are pepperoni.

218. Shredded Wheat was the first breakfast cereal ever produced.

219. Potato chips are the number one selling snack in the United States.

220. Tomatoes were originally thought to be poisonous.

221. If you want to buy a watermelon in Japan, be prepared to pay. They can cost up to $100.

222. An average person's yearly fast food intake will contain 12 pubic hairs.

223. Some vanilla flavorings are made with an ingredient from beaver pee.

CHAPTER 22: GEOGRAPHY

224. The biggest desert in the world is in Antarctica.

225. The water of the Antarctica is so cold that nothing can rot there.

226. An earthquake on Dec. 16, 1811 caused parts of the Mississippi River to flow backwards.

227. If Antarctica's ice sheets melted, the world's oceans would rise by 60 to 65 meters (200 - 210ft) everywhere.

228. The Amazon rainforest produces more than 20 percent of the world's oxygen supply.

229. The warmest temperature ever recorded on Antarctica was 58.3 degrees F.

230. There are more than 50,000 earthquakes throughout the world every year.

231. The state of Florida is bigger than England.

232. The Niagara Falls moves upstream at an average rate of about 295 feet a century.

233. The Dallas/Fort Worth airport is larger than New York City's Manhattan Island.

CHAPTER 23: LAW AND CRIME

234. In 1386, a pig in France was executed by public hanging for the murder of a child.

235. The people most often killed in robberies are the robbers.

236. The United Nations declared the Internet a basic human right in 2011.

237. Every day 20 banks are robbed. The average take is $2,500.

238. The U.S. Government will not allow portraits of living persons to appear on stamps. Usually. It occasionally happens by accident.

239. Only one out of 700 identity thieves gets caught.

240. Nose prints are used to identify dogs, just like humans use fingerprints.

241. Native Americans do not have to pay tax on their land.

242. Most burglaries occur during the daytime.

243. Al Capone's business card said he was a used furniture dealer.

CHAPTER 24: TECH STUFF

244. To have your picture taken by the very first camera you would have had to sit still for 8 hours.

245. Surgeons who grew up playing video games make 37 percent fewer mistakes.

246. Windmills always turn anti-clockwise, except for the windmills in Ireland.

247. The technology contained in a single Gameboy unit in 2000 exceeds all the computing power that was used to put the first man on moon in 1969.

248. Thomas Alva Edison patented almost 1,300 inventions in his lifetime.

249. The first alarm clock could only ring at 4 a.m.

250. The electric chair was invented by a dentist.

251. Originally, Nintendo was a playing card manufacturer.

252. Jumbo jets use 4,000 gallons of fuel to take off.

253. A small airplane can fly backwards.

254. The first "selfie" photograph was taken in 1839 by Robert Cornelius, a chemist who did photography as a hobby..

ACKNOWLEDGEMENTS

First of all, I want to acknowledge my Mom. She's always told me I could be whatever I wanted to be. She bought me my first book about facts and that is what got me interested in them. My sister taught me how to read before I was in kindergarten and everything I am is because of her. My Dad is really smart and I learn a lot of amazing facts from him.

ABOUT THE AUTHOR

Liam Willis is a junior high student and lives in a small rural community east of Dallas, Texas with his mother and sister. 254 Facts you Never Knew is his first book.